Getting Un-Dumped! Your 3-Week Break-Up Recovery Guide

By Joy R. Robinson

Scripture quotations in this book are taken from the New King James Version Copyright©1982 by Thomas Nelson, Inc. Used by permission. All rights reserved.

Getting UnDumped: Your 3-Week Break-Up Recovery Guide

Joy4Life Publishing and Editorial Services LLC
www.joyrrobinson.com

ISBN 978-0-692-83542-5
Copyright© 2016 Joy R. Robinson

Cover by Prodesignsx
Back cover author photo Joy Robinson, hair by Peter Ishmon, Hairistic Perfections by Peter

No part of this book may be reproduced or transmitted in any form or by any means electronic or mechanical—including photocopying, recording, or by any information storage and retrieval system—without permission from the publisher.

Thank you's and Acknowledgments

I would like to thank some very important people in my life without whom this book would not be possible. First, I want to thank the people I call the "Front liners." These are the people who walked through my Getting UnDumped experience first-hand: My sister Melanie Johnson, I love you endlessly! My friends Allen and Linda Stone, Cathryn Veal Harris, Dawn Howland Smith, and Deborah Searle Pennington. Thank you for your genuine love and friendship then, and now.

To my Savannah State University fellow alum Fred Ogletree, thank you for your encouragement, for reading this book and for confirming that there is a powerful message within these pages.

To my friend and brother in Christ, Tremayne Moore, your advice has been invaluable and I owe you so very much! Thank you and bless you in all your publishing endeavors.

To my sister-in-Christ-friend, Apostle Melissia "Mimi" Ewell Pinto, I do not have the space to thank you for your love, support, and encouragement. Thank you, and may God continuously bless you!

To my wonderful children, Justin, Jackie, and Janelle, thank you for your true love and support. Thank you most of all, for believing in your mother.

To my beloved husband Torrey, thank you for loving me! Thank you for hanging in there. Thank you for giving me space for my "writing modes." Thank you for your endless support. I love you!

And most importantly, thank you to my Lord and Savior Jesus Christ. I am nothing without You.

Joy Robinson
January 29, 2017

Contents

Prologue

Week 1: Closure

Week 2: Love

Week 3: Wisdom

Epilogue

Appendix

Blessed be the God and Father of our Lord Jesus Christ, the Father of mercies and God of all comfort, who comforts us in all our tribulation, that we may be able to comfort those who are in any trouble, with the comfort with which we ourselves are comforted by God.

2 Corinthians 1:3-4

Prologue

It was not my first break-up, nor was it my last. But it was THE break-up that birthed the book you now hold in your hands. In fact, it was the biggest break-up since my divorce and you would think that after something as major as a divorce, the ending of a minor relationship would not be so devastating. The truth is that relationships ending after a divorce are more devastating than relationships prior to the divorce. That was certainly true of me. Why? Because I was trying to prove that I was wife material. That I was worthy to be married. That I could be a good wife and if I could convince my man at that time, surely the proposal of my dreams would follow. But…that didn't exactly work out. After a year of dating, he.dumped.me. Insert flatline here.

I was furious. I was devastated. I was confused. I was lost. And then, I made a decision. I was not going to spend several months to a year wallowing in despair and mourning my loss. I mean after all, it was *his* loss, right? (Yeah, we'll talk more about that later.) So, I gave myself a time limit. I literally looked at my calendar and marked out 21 days— 3 weeks that I would I allow myself to process this year-long relationship and then I would be done. I was not intending to write a book. I really wasn't trying to share my humiliation. All I wanted to do was repair my broken heart, get back on my feet, and move on. But I knew I needed a plan. Going out clubbing with my girlfriends was not a plan. Drinking myself to sleep every night was not a plan. Besides, I had already tried that going through the divorce. No, this time I wanted real healing and no residue. I thought that I was in one of my most emotionally healthy states *before* this relationship, and I was angry that this relationship had depleted me and left me worse than I was at the beginning. I just wanted to get back to that secure, confident, empowered woman that I once was. What developed from that one decision is what you are about to read and the journey you are about to embark upon.

Break-ups can be very treacherous waters to navigate, especially if you don't have guidance. If you're like me, many times I ended up in a worse mental state after the break-up, than being in the middle of a bad relationship. The truth is, when a relationship ends, you do suffer a loss to some degree. But, the good news is that some very positive things can come from a break up including a healthier mental state, an opportunity for a better relationship, and most importantly, life lessons that can empower you and propel you into your best life.

The advice in this book implements a three-week relationship pause after you experience a break-up. During this time, I ask that you diligently refrain from entering a new dating relationship. This is very important. My desire is that you heal from your past relationship so you can walk into a new relationship healthier, wiser, and better. If you jump into a new relationship too soon, your chances of being successful will be less. In addition, you should avoid communicating with your ex. Don't look shocked. I'm not saying you all can't get back together, later. Much, much later. But right now, rehearsing your relationship, what he/she did wrong, where did it fall apart, begging for a second chance, or being mad that they are not begging you for a second chance serve no purpose in your journey to healing. Seeking the answers to your questions from your ex most likely won't bring you any closer to understanding. What you need now is clarity, safety, and an emotional break in order to find the truth. If you and your ex are truly destined to be together, they will still be there three weeks from now. So wouldn't it be better if YOU are emotionally healthier then?

Lastly, I ask that you acquire a notebook or journal for your recovery journey. Doesn't have to be really big---remember this is only a three-week process, but you will need it to write out your exercises and homework that will help you get UnDumped! And while you may be tempted to rush through this short manual in a few days, I strongly urge you to take the full 21 days allotted for this process. It may seem like a short period of time, but this journey is designed for you to maximize each day, even if it's just a mental health day.

*This book is NOT intended for married couples going through divorce.

Closure

Week 1: Be Sure the Relationship is Over and Be Sure of Why

Things were going great. Or, so I thought. We had made it to a year! No, everything wasn't perfect. We never talked about marriage, and I didn't bring it up because…well…I didn't want to pressure him and I figured he already knew that was what I really wanted. But for the most part, we had a cool relationship. He had taken me to meet his family. I met his sons. He had met my children. We went out dancing and to eat and to watch football and baseball games. He sent me a "Good morning Sweetheart," text every morning without fail. And he was the last person I spoke to every night. He told all his friends and co-workers about me. When we went to the company cookout, they all knew who I was. Especially the women. But Christmas came, and no ring. The one-year mark was quickly passing and there was no discussion about our forever. I was getting nervous. Anxious. Paranoid. Irritable. And then in one seemingly normal conversation something snapped. He had been avoiding committing to spending time with me that week and I was growing more and more impatient. All of my friends, who had barely seen me for a year, were wondering when we were going to get hitched. I had always been suspicious of his rather-friendly relationship with his ex-wife. And his ex-fiancée had called my phone to "warn" me about him. But I was holding on for dear life. I thought if I showed him how loyal I was, he would propose. So, that afternoon when we were talking on the phone and he was not giving me the answers I wanted to hear, I snapped. I started venting all the pent-up anxiety and frustration that I had been holding for the last several months. My voice went into unnatural octaves. The words were flying out of my mouth at 100 miles per hour. And in my mind, I thought it was about time I set him straight and now he could get his act together.

Well, then he snapped.

He was angry, frustrated, and fed-up. And in about five minutes, we were done. He did not disrespect me or call me any names. He just said, "I don't want to do this anymore." My knees buckled. My heart cracked. No no no no no no no no no!!!! This was not what I wanted! This was not what I was trying to get. I immediately began begging. "Please," I cried. I sobbed. He hung up the phone. I slid to the floor of my kitchen and cried my eyes out.

I was sure the relationship was over, but I wasn't clear on why. Later, he came over and we tried to talk. I was almost too angry to speak.

What had I done wrong? I had bent over backwards to keep him happy. I was always fresh and looking good when we went out. I did not ask him for money. I did not try to control him. I did not nag him about hanging out with his guy friends. I had listened to him vent about work and I supported his relationships with his sons. His youngest son did not like me but I didn't try to force myself on the boy. What was wrong with me? "You didn't do anything wrong," he said. "You're a phenomenal lady," he said. "Oh really? Then why are you breaking-up with me?" I shot back. And then softer, "I thought we were going to get married."

"Have you ever heard me talk about getting married?" he asked. "Did I ever say anything about moving in with you or making any type of plans?" No, he had not. Not at all.

He apologized repeatedly. He wished me the best. We had plans for New Year's Eve which I made him promise to keep with me--I did not want to spend New Year's Eve alone—and then he would be free of me. We went out dancing to bring in the new year. We toasted at midnight. He gave me one final kiss, and we were done. Back home alone, I was in a permanent fetal position. I posted on Facebook "If you love me at all, pray for me." I struggled through the days like trying to swim in quick sand. My friends called to check on me. They invited me out and thankfully, I went. They told me he had messed up. That he had made the biggest mistake of his life. I listened to all of that, but I still did not understand why he dumped me. It just didn't make sense. The more I tried to figure it out, the more frustrated I became, building up into full blown anger. By the time I went to back to work after the holiday, my anger was venomous. I was angry about the break-up. I was angry that I had wasted a year of my life, thinking we were going to get married. And I was angry about the prospect of having to be that dumped, broken, single-mom for some unknown period of time waiting for a knight-in-shinning-armor to rescue me from the dungeon of singleness purgatory.

  I had read somewhere that it takes 21 days to break an old habit and start a new one. That was it, I decided. I looked at my calendar and marked out 21 days that I would allow myself to be angry and sad and then I would wash my hands of my ex and all the negative emotions with him. I was not going to carry a broken heart for months-on-end waiting for someone new to come along. I was healthy, happy, and single *before* him. I wasn't even looking for a relationship! I was not about to get stuck now. I didn't have a specific tool to guide me, but I knew from going through my divorce that I needed to purge the negative emotions I was feeling. I needed to put the pieces of my heart back together and breathe again.

Day 1: Angry/Cry Day

About a week after this break-up I was back at work and boiling on the inside. Being a teacher I absolutely had to contain my rage so throughout the day I bombarded my ex with text messages telling him all the things I was angry about. For a full 24-hour period, every time I thought of something that set me off, I sent him a text and let him have it! Poor guy. Thankfully, the man never responded to my tirade. I was having a virtual temper tantrum. I was furious—mostly with myself, but we will discuss that later. If he had responded, it would have been a far worse situation. Now if you have or are going through a breakup I am NOT suggesting that you pummel your ex with angry text messages. Don't call and leave a nasty voicemail. Do not send a venomous email. But I highly recommend that you do get a notebook and write. Every angry thought you feel about your ex and about your relationship write it in your journal. (I give specific instructions for this in today's activity.)

What I learned is the importance of expressing the pain of your loss. Too often in relationships, people try to minimize the loss or the anger they feel about a break-up. Well-meaning friends and family may say things to you like "It's their loss," or "They will miss you later," in an attempt to comfort you. But I can tell you from experience that these cover-ups only prevent true, deep healing. When you minimize your pain and loss, you put a band-aid on a wound that is far deeper than that. You are essentially concealing the wound, and covered wounds do not heal.

Look at it. If you hurt yourself and needed to go to the doctor, the doctor would have to look at your wound to determine the best treatment for your healing and recovery. As you write out your "I am angry because and/or I am sad because…statements, my hope is that you will closely examine what is the source of your pain. I know you're thinking, *I'm in pain because I'm not in a relationship anymore!* I know and I truly understand. But I also know that no relationship break-up is that simple. There are layers of dysfunction, or miscommunication, or misalignment of ideals that contribute to the break-up and these areas are the roots of anger and sadness. Underneath red hot anger is always deep hurt. It is necessary to look at what you are angry about so that you can discover the wounds you need to heal. So, let's look at what you are angry or sad about.

Day 1 Action: Write out what you're angry about. Complete this sentence "I am angry because…" Write the sentence as many times as necessary to fully flush out your feelings. Don't worry about being fair to the other person. Don't worry about who is right or who is wrong. Just write how you feel as clearly and specifically as you can. Use as much paper as you need. Try to expose as much about your relationship that you are angry/upset about that you can. ***Caution*** Don't post these thoughts on social media or have an ex-bashing session with your friends. Number one, that only opens the door for people to be all in your business. You may think that people will sympathize with you and give you some type of uplifting, validating feedback that will make you feel better. But this is really an unhealthy coping strategy. Number two, the saying "misery loves company" is true. With social media today, people love to co-sign on negativity of any kind. You will probably get a lot of likes on your post about how angry you are with your ex, but that will only feed your bitterness, and that will prevent your true healing. Bitterness is like plaque build-up on your teeth; eventually it separates your teeth from your gums. In the same way, bitterness separates you from dealing with what the real issues are and ultimately keeps you in a state of brokenness. Perpetual brokenness is not an acceptable way of living. If you had a car that was in the repair shop more than it was on the road running, wouldn't that be a problem? So, it is the same with your heart. Remember you are on a journey to getting un-dumped and getting true healing.

Covered wounds do not heal...

Day 2: Underneath anger is hurt.

If you didn't care about someone, you most likely would not get angry about anything that they say or do. But when someone matters to you, when your whole world revolves around them, you tend to get angry rather quickly when things between you and this person turn sour. That anger is the signifying clue to the depth of your hurt. In my big break-up relationship, I was angry that I had "wasted a year" with that person. I expected that my investment would turn into a marriage and when it was clear that was not going to happen, that is where my hurt was found.

Expressing anger has been the socially accepted emotion for men. Women can be sad, hurt, happy, depressed, *and* angry while men are allowed *only* to be angry---if they are a "real man." Real men possess every single emotion and the capacity to express them that women do. The problem is the restrictions that have been placed on men through generations of social manipulation have created this emotional box that leaves a limited range of feelings for males. As such is the case, it is key to pay attention to the anger that men display. Anger is designed to motivate righteous action. To correct a wrong. To make a U-turn. To set the record straight. Consider then, that an angry man, is a hurt man. A wounded man who deeply desires to correct a wrong; make a U-turn; set the record straight.

How you handle your anger is essential to your healing process. Holding on to anger will not protect you from future hurt. Pretending you are not angry will not make it go away. You must uncover the hurt beneath the anger to see the direction that anger is pointing you to. Acknowledging the hurt beneath the anger validates your feelings even if it is to only yourself. As you do, the healing process will begin.

Day 2 Action: Look back at your anger statements from yesterday. Try to identify the hurt beneath each one. What was it that you expected that did not happen? What was it that you were disappointed about? What dream did you have that is now lost? You may need some tissues for this, but it's okay. You may have to pause and breathe as you reflect, and that is truly okay. Take the time to turn your "I am angry about…" statements into "I am hurt because…" statements. Write these out in your journal so that you can look at them and see where the wounds are that need to be healed. Uncovering the hurt is essential to getting undumped and the first big step to getting healing in your heart.

Day 3: Forgiveness Day 1

So, I had given myself 24 hours to be angry and to vent my anger. As I said, I unleashed my anger through text messages upon my ex, and I am NOT recommending that you do that! Your ex may not be as gracious as mine was to not reply, or come after me. After a full day of anger, it was time for forgiveness. The next day, I literally went back into the text messages I had sent him and changed them to say "I forgive you for…" in front of whatever I had previously said I was angry about, and pressed SEND. Yes, I really did. He didn't respond to those texts either, at first. I am sure he thought I was crazy. Later, he thanked me for forgiving him, but that wasn't the reason I sent the "I forgive you for…" texts. What he probably didn't realize is something I really want you to understand. I was forgiving him to retrieve my mental and emotional power. With every forgiveness statement, I was really saying to him *I am taking back my feelings, my affections, my emotions, my mental space and I am standing in my own skin, independent of you.* I needed to forgive him so that there would be nothing in me that could be later triggered and then drag me back to a place of hurt and anger. I did not want to hear an old song that we used to dance to and feel hurt.

I did not want to avoid restaurants that we had gone to. I did not want to live in pain and avoidance, so I had to forgive him. It's like a remote control car. There is a transmitter inside the car that responds to the outside remote control. Whatever the person holding that controller does, affects and controls the car. You cannot afford to not have control of your emotions.

Unforgiveness leaves the control in the hands of the person you have not forgiven. In the worst-case scenario, when he/she knows they still have you on their hook, they can use that to manipulate you---like the car controller. Some people will manipulate you to get something they want from you. Some people will manipulate you just for the emotional rise they get out of you. Some people will manipulate you for nothing more than bragging rights and jokes. On the other hand, the person you haven't forgiven may go on with their life, leaving you alone, not thinking about you or bothering you in any way, but your unforgiveness keeps you in bondage. And this is a stealth, but more deadly type of control. This type of control blocks you from a new, healthy relationship and keeps you in perpetual brokenness. Perpetual brokenness is not your portion, Beloved.

Forgiveness is not easy to just do. I know you're thinking that! You are probably thinking "Joy, you just don't know what they did! It is unforgiveable." I don't want you to think that I could forgive my ex just that easily either. But by sending those forgiveness texts, I started the process. It was an announcement I made to my heart that I was not going to live in bondage, fear, or depression. I would be free from pain, and forgiveness was the key to my liberation.

Day 3 Action: Write out your forgiveness statements. Take the "I am hurt because…" statements, which were your "I am angry about…" statements, and put "I forgive you for…" in front of them. Say them out loud. Breathe in before you say the sentence, and then exhale when you finish. Involve your entire body in the process. Surrender to forgiveness. Repeat the forgiveness statements standing in front of a mirror so that you can see yourself forgiving your ex. If you start to cry, go ahead and cry. But don't listen to the voice telling you that forgiveness means that what they did was okay. Don't' believe the lie that you can't forgive them if they don't apologize. An apology is not necessary for you to forgive them. Closure happens when you close the door. Stop waiting on someone to give you closure. You are not forgiving them for them. You are forgiving them for you.

Day 4: Mental Health Day

When I literally went through this, I obviously did not have this book to guide me, so I did not have the daily activities already planned. But by the middle of the first week, I was mentally and emotionally drained. I did not want to think about this anymore. I did not want to be sad or angry. I just didn't want to feel anything. I did not want to talk to anyone about it. I just wanted and needed a mental holiday from all of it. And that's exactly what I did.

I tend to over analyze things, to a fault. I guess it's a part of my personality. The problem with that is it's very hard for me to shut my brain off. And when there is a problem I am facing, I really over think! This was the pattern I had gotten into with this breakup. My mind kept dissecting the same questions repeatedly: Why did he dump me? What did I do wrong? Could I have done anything different? Was he ever telling me the truth? Is this just me getting what I deserve because of my failed marriage? Am I ever going to be in a happy relationship? Are there any good men out there? And the list went on. Every waking moment. And late into the night.

I didn't know then that this was the classic anxiety-depression cycle, but I did know that I needed to take a break. So, on Day 4 I took a mental health day. You may have heard people use this term on your job. It is when you take the "day off" from your job or whatever situation that is high stress or anxiety for you. You do not think about, talk about, or try to resolve anything related to the stressor, in this case your ex and the breakup. You release your mind from the constraints of wrestling with the issue and focus your thinking power elsewhere. You clear your mental space to make room for the positive aspects of your life. The Apostle Paul, who went through extreme rejection and persecution, said it this way,

> *Finally, brethren, whatever things are true, whatever things are noble, whatever things are just, whatever things are pure, whatever things are lovely, whatever things of good report, if there is any virtue and if there is anything praiseworthy—meditate on these things. Philippians 4:8*

Day 4 Action: Don't believe everything you think. Release your mind from the regimen of analyzing your breakup and condemning your ex. Choose the direction of your mental state today by choosing to elevate your thoughts over your current situation. Get up and get out, or stay in and relax. Either way the goal is to not use your mental powers for overanalyzing your breakup, you, your ex, or any of the "what if" scenarios floating around in your head. Instead just breathe, rest, and repeat for today. For 24-hours. You can do anything for one day. You will be glad you did.

Turn your mind off and take a mental health day.

Day 5: Acknowledge your part in the breakdown of the relationship.

The truth is, I was just as much to blame for the breakdown of the relationship as my ex. When we met, he was in a failing relationship with another woman. They were engaged to be married, but when I questioned why he did not seem excited about their upcoming nuptials, he poured out his heart. He was conflicted because of resentment and fear. I told him they had to talk about it. I reminded him that she loved him and that he loved her, otherwise they would not be engaged. I encouraged him to get counseling and I tried to help him understand a woman's perspective on things. What I realized later, is that with every piece of advice I gave him, his attraction to me was building because in his mind he was comparing her to me. He never crossed the line and neither did I, but then without any warning, he told me that he had broken up with her and had called off the wedding. Now, we talked much more often. Daily. Several times a day. For a couple of hours. The next thing I knew we were out to dinner together. And this is where my part in the breakdown of the relationship really began. I knew we were heading into a relationship and I knew he was not ready—emotionally unavailable—and I chose to ignore that.

I shouldn't have been in a relationship with this guy in the first place. Now of course all along the way, I continued to build my own fantasy world around the misconceptions I chose to tell myself. The signs were all there but I wanted to be in a relationship so badly. Even though I knew he wasn't 100% in, I clung to the belief that I could convince him to fully commit by being loyal, tolerant, and patient. My contribution to the breakdown and eventual blow-up of the relationship was the illusion that I created in my own head that he was not willing to live out.

What was your part in the breakdown of your relationship? Don't automatically dismiss this question and tell yourself that it was all their fault. I am not telling you to take responsibility for their behavior. If they cheated on you or lied to you, for example, those are actions they chose and are not your fault, I don't care what they say. No one can make someone cheat on them. No amount of maintenance can prevent someone from cheating if that person is not committed to being loyal themselves. Ladies, you cannot sex him enough to keep him from cheating on you. Men, you cannot spend enough money on her to keep her from cheating. Free yourself from taking on burdens that are not yours. But I am asking you to own your stuff. Were you judgmental, disrespectful, or inconsiderate? Did you have expectations that he/she was not aware of and then crucify them when they did not meet your expectations? Did you demand a standard of treatment for yourself that you withheld from your ex? Were you the one who was not 100% committed and when they finally realized it they dumped you? Be honest. With yourself.

Day 5 Action: In your journal, acknowledge your part in the breakdown of the relationship. You must admit it to yourself in order to be able to change it and grow from it. It is a simple but profound exercise. Make a list of the actions and/or non-actions you took that contributed to the meltdown and breakup. Don't worry if the list is short or long. For each item, identify your motive behind the action. Was it fear? Anger? Lack of information? Did you really think you were doing the right thing but now you can see that it was a wrong turn? Write that down too. When you are finished, step back (figuratively speaking) and look at it. Do you see any patterns of behavior? Do you see any connections to your past, pervious relationships, or an underlying belief you have? Do you see anything that you need to forgive yourself for? Good. Turn the page.

Day 6: Forgiveness Day 2 Accepting Forgiveness

One of the most important things we forget to do during or after a break up (and in life in general) is to forgive ourselves. In my own life, I have unknowingly held a grudge against myself for mistakes that I have made and then when I finally sat down to think about it, I realized that I was angry and needed to forgive myself. On Day 5, I acknowledged my part in the breakup and blowup of the relationship. Now I needed to forgive myself for it. I had to forgive myself for ignoring the red flags that told me he was not ready to be in a relationship. I had to forgive myself for thinking I could persuade him to marry me. I had to forgive myself for sacrificing my life, joy, peace, and rest trying to prove that I was worthy to be married. I had to forgive myself for not having the courage to dump him, instead of waiting for him to dump me.

But let me tell you that self-forgiveness is a bit more difficult to apply than forgiving someone else. In truth, it is rather impossible without assistance. The ability to forgive comes from the transforming power of *being forgiven*, and that must come from experiencing forgiveness through Jesus Christ. Up until this point in this book I have asked you to do things that for the most part you can do on your own, difficult though they may be. But I want to pause here and introduce to you the truth around which Getting UnDumped is centered. The truth is no man or woman can un-break your heart; only Jesus can do that, because He was broken for you. The truth is that you are best able to forgive yourself and anyone else, when you have received God's forgiveness of you. Forgiveness is best when re-gifted. So how do you do that?

According to the Bible, the Word of God, in the book of First John, chapter 1, verse 9 it says, *"If we confess our sins, He is faithful and righteous to forgive us our sins and to cleanse us from all unrighteousness."* You may be asking yourself, "What did I do wrong? I was just trying to love someone and be loved in return." I understand that. But a critical part of your healing is your ability to forgive them, and forgive yourself, <u>but you can only get the power to do that by accepting forgiveness from God through Jesus Christ</u>. Maybe you have never thought about your life in this way. Maybe you have never made the connection between the state of your soul and your relationship status. Maybe you have never understood the story of how mankind fell into sin and how God implemented a plan to redeem and save us. Yes, us! Me and you! When Adam and Eve, the first people God made sinned, it caused all humans to be born in a state of sin. This state of sin came with a penalty of death and eternal separation from God. But God had a plan of redemption for humans and that plan was his Son, Jesus Christ taking the death penalty in our place. Over two thousand years ago, Jesus who was sinless, was crucified for you and me. And now, through faith, we can accept the offer of salvation and forgiveness of our sinful state. When you receive salvation, you are born-again. Your spirit is made alive in Christ because your sinful nature is dead in Christ. If you want to be made whole, if you want your heart to be truly healed, if you want to get undumped, then the best way to do that is to make Jesus your personal Savior and the Lord of your life. All it takes is three simple steps:

1. Confess your sinful state and ask for forgiveness. Say this: God, I admit I am a sinner and I need your help. I ask for your forgiveness through your son Jesus Christ.
2. Make Jesus your personal Savior and the Lord of your life. Say: Jesus I believe that you died for my sins and rose again and through your shed blood I am saved.
3. Tell someone you just got saved! Find a Bible-teaching Christian church to attend and join. Get involved in the church. Pray every day and read the Bible every day.

If you just received Christ as your Savior and became born again, let me be the first to say CONGRATULATIONS!!!

Day 6 Action: If you are already a Christian, maybe you need to refresh your commitment to Him. Maybe you are like I was and got so caught up in the relationship that I got off track and made some major mistakes. The beautiful thing about God is that He allows U-turns. He will take you wherever you are and help you walk the path to restoration and life. There is nothing you can do to mess up so badly that God will not take you back. He is waiting on you. If you need to repent and recommit to God say this: *Father, I confess my sins to you. I am nothing without you. Please forgive me, restore me and heal my heart. I thank you for hearing and answering my prayer, in Jesus' name. Amen.*

If you are a new Christian or a restored Christian, I want to hear from you! Go to www.joyrrobinson.com to send me an email (more details in Appendix A).

And now my friend, we must continue our journey to healing and Getting UnDumped. Oh no, it's not over yet, but I want to say congratulations on making it this far. Emotional matters are some of the most difficult to navigate, but it is worth it if you want to be whole. Being whole gives you the best chance of your next relationship being healthier and more rewarding. So, let us continue with your new or renewed relationship with Christ as the source of your strength and healing.

Closure happens when YOU close the door. Stop waiting for your ex to give you closure.

Day 7 Forgiveness Day 3 Forgiving Yourself

Now, getting back to forgiveness. Go back into your journal and find the page where you wrote out your part in the breakdown of the relationship. Now it's time to put "I forgive myself for…" in front of those statements. One of the things I had to ask for forgiveness of God for and forgive myself for was having sex with that guy and thinking that would help convince him to marry me. Sex outside of marriage is a sin and now that you are a born-again believer, this is a truth you must live by. Don't get all depressed if you've been a little promiscuous, or very promiscuous. God forgives it all. You must repent (admit it, and commit to not living that way anymore) and allow God to help you live righteously from now on. You don't have to get yourself all cleaned up and together by yourself. God will help you. All you have to do is accept His help.

Day 7 Action: Just like when you forgave your ex and you spoke out loud your "I forgive you for…" statements, now do the same for yourself. Breathe in before you say each sentence, and then exhale when you finish. Involve your entire body in the process. Allow your heart to forgive your soul. Repeat the forgiveness statements continuously until it becomes solidified in your heart and mind. Until you feel your mood lifting. Until you see light at the end of the tunnel. Until…you believe it.

Remember this, forgiveness is a never-ending process. It is actually a cycle that is vital to your survival in life. First, you accept forgiveness from God and this gives you the grace to forgive yourself, which in turn empowers you to forgive others. And you go through this cycle regularly, daily if need be. All successful relationships include a component of forgiveness. Friendships, business partnerships, and romantic relationships all need forgiveness. Otherwise, no relationship would last very long.

Forgiving is not a prerequisite for salvation. It is a post-salvation benefit.

I'm Not Where You Left Me

Excuse me, did you lose someone?
Yes. Yes, you did
And it was on purpose.

We started out together
Hand in Hand embrace

But you left me...

Left me for dead
Left me to die
Left me alone, though you promised to be there
Left me in the cold
Left me starving
Left me bruised
Left me burned, nearly charred
Left
Left
Left, Right
Left,
Right after a little joy, and all the pain
Right after I gave what I could not regain
Right in the middle of the dream that was really a lie...

But unlike things, people who are left
With legs to walk,
And God on their side,
Do not stay where they are left.

~JRR

Love

Week 2: Remind yourself of God's endless love for you.

Day 8: God loves you more than any human ever could, or ever will.

I had gotten accustomed to the daily "Good morning," texts from my ex. He was speaking my love language! I would lay in bed awake waiting for his text to come through. Faithfully, between 6:00am and 6:15am, his personalized tone would ring and that was the sunshine to my whole day. I could get up then, and get my day started with a smile. It literally flipped a switch inside me that gave me the energy to get out of bed. But after the break-up, there were no more "good morning" texts. I fell into instant depression. I could not get out of the bed. I felt like I had no reason to. I felt unloved. I felt broken. I felt like a used paper towel that was thrown away. What was I going to do now?

One of the biggest mistakes people make after a break-up is to try to replace that lost love with a new love right away. People say things like "The best way to get over someone is with someone else." In the days and weeks after being dumped, I did want to find someone who would love me for real. Obviously, the guy did not really love me even though he said he did, so I just needed to find "true love." That would solve the problem, right? Wrong.

What is true love anyway? So many people think they have found it in that one special person but then something happens and what they thought was true love is anything but true. It is a frustrating quest. And when that once true love is gone, you are left with a big, gaping hole in your heart. We have all heard at some point in our lives that God loves us. We see it on cards, bumper stickers, t-shirts, and even commercials inviting people to church. For me personally, I grew up in the church and have a solid foundation of understanding the Bible but like many, many people I didn't really believe that God's love could satisfy my need for human love. I knew God loved me enough to send his Son to die for me and save me, but I had not really applied that love to my broken-heart. I thought of God's love for me like a parent-child relationship and I really felt that romantic relationships were just a human condition that God didn't really get deeply involved in.

There is a hierarchy of love types that we need to understand in order to receive the healing we need. According to the ancient Greeks, there are four different types of love and each type has different characteristics that make it unique from the others. The four types of love are Agape, Storge, Phileo, and Eros. Agape is the highest form of love. It is God in essence. Eros is the human, erotic love. It is the lowest form of love and yet it is the one type of love that we seek and desire the most. A good way to think of Storge is the parent-to-child love, or cousin-to-cousin love. It is a love that seems to naturally occur between family members. Phileo is brotherly love. The people don't have to be related to each other. It's that BFF type of love. It is important to understand all of these different forms of love, but I want to focus here on Agape love and the sharp contrast between Agape and Eros.

Eros is affection that is erotic in nature and is largely based on emotions and body chemistry. The object of Eros love is external, but the motivation is internal. Eros love says "I love you because you make me happy." Usually, this is the type of love that exists between couples and when combined with the other three types of love is not a bad thing. Married couples should absolutely have Eros love and God created marriage for the safe consumption of Eros. But when Eros love becomes the primary and only type of love in a relationship there are grave consequences. In truth, this type of love is conditional. If or when the object of your affection ceases to do or be what you fell in love with, then Eros love falters. Typically, this is where a break-up occurs and someone gets dumped.

In contrast, Agape love is true unconditional love. Agape is the substance of God's make-up. It is His DNA. You could spend years studying the nature of God, the nature of Agape love, and still never understand it all. But for the purpose of your healing and getting undumped, there are a few characteristics we need to look at. Agape love is:

- *unconditional.* There is nothing you can do to earn it.
- *endless.* There is nothing you can do to end it.
- the only love-type that has *healing powers.*

In the Bible, Jesus tells a story that beautifully demonstrates how Agape love heals a broken heart. In Luke chapter 10, verse 30, Jesus begins:

> *"A certain man went down from Jerusalem to Jericho, and fell among thieves, who stripped him of his clothing, wounded him, and departed, leaving him half dead."*

The man traveling was going from Jerusalem to Jericho, a 17-mile trip where theft attacks were common. Sometimes relationships can seem like this treacherous 17-mile journey! The thieves stripped the man of his clothes, wounded him, and left him half dead. After getting dumped I felt like I had been stripped, wounded, and left for dead. My boundaries of trust were violated and my vulnerability was exposed. I was undoubtedly wounded---broken-hearted. And even though he did it respectfully, I was dumped and left alone. Emotionally, I felt like the man in Jesus' story. Two other travelers passed by the wounded man and did not offer to help him, but thankfully a good Samaritan came along.

> *"And when he saw him, he had compassion. So he went to him and bandaged his wounds, pouring on oil and wine; and he set him on his own animal, brought him to an inn, and took care of him." Luke 10:33-34*

Where the man was naked, the Samaritan covered him. Where the man was injured, the Samaritan attended to his wounds. Where the man was left to die, the Samaritan picked him up and brought him to safety. In ancient times, wine was used as an antiseptic to prevent infection, and oil was used as both a lubricant and protective barrier. What the good Samaritan did was the definition of Agape love. The Samaritan did not know the victim. They were not related. The victim did not have any way to pay the Samaritan for his services, and yet the Samaritan showed the highest level of love, Agape love. This is how God loves us through a break-up. This is how God heals us from a break-up. This is how we get undumped.

Day 8 Action: Remember how I told you the daily "Good morning" texts from my ex made my day and literally empowered me to get out of bed? Well after the breakup, I had to replace that daily so-called love deposit with something more real. There is nothing more real than the love of God for you and He expresses that explicitly in His Word. The problem was, I had allowed my boyfriend to take priority in my life in a very unhealthy way. It is perfectly fine and natural to look forward to and enjoy daily communication with your significant other, however when their words are higher than God's Word in your life, it creates an imbalance that contaminates the relationship, and can contribute to a breakup. Like a natural diet, I needed to replace what I had been feeding on, the words of man, with God's Word and God's love for me. After getting dumped, I struggled with getting out of bed every morning, and I suffered from insomnia at night. The solution to this problem was and still is praying and reading the Bible regularly. During my break-up recovery, I decided to implement a daily routine that would help me heal. Instead of waiting for a "Good morning" text, I chose to turn to the true source of love, God, in prayer. On the next page, I share with you the prayers I wrote that I prayed daily, one in the morning, and one at night. I encourage you to pray these prayers as well, each day for the rest of this 21-day journey. I also share some of the key scriptures that were the "oil and wine" poured into my heart to heal me. I believe in taking the Word of God like medicine for my soul and I believe it will greatly help you as well. Today's scriptures accompanied by some reflection questions are here:

1. Cause me to hear Your loving-kindness in the morning, for in You do I trust; Cause me to know the way in which I should walk, for I lift up my soul to You. (NKJV) Psalm 143:8
In your journal answer, **what does God's loving-kindness in the morning look like or sound like to you?**

2. I would have lost heart, unless I had believed that I would see the goodness of the Lord in the land of the living. Wait on the Lord; Be of good courage, and He shall strengthen your heart; Wait I say on the Lord! (NKJV) Psalm 27:13-14
In your journal answer, **what is the "goodness" that you are believing God to see while you are alive?**

3. For I am persuaded that neither death nor life, nor angels nor principalities nor powers, nor things to come, nor height nor depth, nor any other created thing, shall be able to separate us from the love of God which is in Christ Jesus our Lord. (NKJV) Romans 8:38-39
In your journal answer, **if there is nothing that can separate you from the love of God, how does that impact the way you live and think every day?**

He sent His word and healed them, and delivered them from their destructions. Psalm 107:20

Morning Prayer

Thank you Father for this beautiful day that you have made! I will rejoice and be glad TODAY! Before I set foot outside my door, I acknowledge that you God are the source of my strength. For it is in you that I live, and breathe and have my being. I am complete in you. I invite you Holy Spirit to monitor and influence all that I think, say, and do today. I ask for your guidance and wisdom in all the circumstances, and situations that I will face today. Empower me Lord, to exemplify your love toward every person that I will interact with today. Bless them, and let their day be richer because they will have encountered YOU through ME. Empower me to work in your spirit of excellence. Enable me to be creative, innovative, wise, and exquisite. Lead me by your spirit in the path that I should walk today. Be a fence of protection around me and my loved ones. Please remind me that you are with me today...and, always. Thank you again Jesus for your love, your grace, and your favor TODAY.

Evening Prayer

Thank you Father for another day that you have blessed me to live. It was by your grace that I was victorious in all my endeavors today. Thank you Lord for your wisdom, guidance, and protection in every situation that I faced today. I entrust this day and all that took place in it into your hands Lord. I forfeit any glory to my name and give all glory and honor to You. Today I walked in my destiny and I thank you Jesus for walking with me. Forgive me Father, for where I made a misstep. Teach me to avoid these distractions and pitfalls in the future. And now, I forgive all those who sinned against me today. I release the hurt and anger. I exhale all negativity. I embrace forgiveness entirely. I lay all my concerns at your nail-scarred feet Jesus. I believe that you died to redeem and rectify every one of my issues. I receive Your peace now as I lay down to sleep. My mind will rest in the knowledge that my life is in your hands God, and you are in control. Restore, refresh and renew my mind, body, and spirit as I sleep tonight Lord. Be a fence of protection around me and my loved ones throughout the night. Thank you for the forgiveness of my sins. Thank you for the promise of eternal life with you.

> *The Lord is near to those who have a broken heart, and saves such as have a contrite spirit. Psalm 34:18*

Day 9: You are complete in Him.

In the movie, Jerry Maguire, Tom Cruise utters the now infamous words "You complete me," to his love interest. Over time, this line came to be the mantra for people looking for love---they were looking for someone to "complete" them in the way that Tom Cruise meant it in the movie. Since then though, some people have awakened to the fact that this idea of completing someone isn't such a good idea. If you need someone to complete you, then that implies that you are somehow inadequate, insufficient, and lacking. More and more relationship experts are speaking out about this and saying that a person needs to be whole all by themselves before they are ready for a relationship with another person. To a certain degree, I agree with this. But after my break-up, I struggled with feeling incomplete now that my guy was gone.

We live in a society designed for couples. Everything from 2 for $20 meal deals, to bonus "buddy passes" for events and trips are designed with two people in mind, not a single person. If you're like me, you greatly desire to be in a couple unit. You want to function and move around in your world as part of a "we" that is greater than "you" by yourself. How wonderful does it feel to go out to a movie, or to dinner, or just to the store, with your loved one? How comforting to hold their hand, or feel them rubbing your back? But when you are single the pain of their absence is excruciating. When I was dumped, I despised seeing other couples. They were everywhere and they seemed so much happier than I could ever be. Even at my wonderful church, couples would hold hands during worship service and it took everything in me not to vomit! The embers of anger were stirring up within me and I had no choice but to go to God about it. "Why are you torturing me God?" I asked. "I feel like a lost puzzle piece," I sobbed in the shower where I usually cried so my children would not hear me. Thankfully, His soft, gentle voice spoke to me, "You are complete IN ME." Where had I heard that before? Colossians 2:10 says *"...and you are complete in Him, who is the head of all principality and power."*

    I had to marinate on that for a while. I mean this isn't exactly what I was trying to say to God. I knew God loves me and wants the best for me but I had a hard time picturing God taking me out on a date or physically holding my hand. God's love saved my soul, but I needed a man to make me feel complete here on earth…or so I thought. A common piece of advice given to singles is to get comfortable being with yourself. Take yourself out on a date. Take yourself to dinner. And it makes sense…in theory. But who wants to go out to eat alone? Not me! The idea is to not be dependent on having a girlfriend/boyfriend in order to enjoy life. But what ends up happening is people go out alone only to add another traumatic experience to their psyche because being complete is a process that God does inside you, not just the ability to go to a restaurant and endure the agony of eating a meal alone. So how did I do it? How did I get to the point where I am very comfortable treating myself to breakfast, lunch, or dinner by myself? There are a few epiphanies I had to realize, and so do you.

1. When you go out alone, people don't see you the same way you see you unless you tell them. I had to realize that I did not have a big "L" for loser plastered on my forehead that everyone could see every time I stepped out of my door. I knew I had just gotten out of a relationship but strangers at my favorite restaurant did not know that. They were not whispering about how pitiful it was that I had to take myself out to eat. They were not reviewing the record of mistakes I made to cause my ex to dump me. Furthermore, no one would know unless I told them. I learned to stop introducing myself with my relationship status. You know, when people ask you to tell them a little about yourself and you start with, "Well, I just got out of a bad relationship so…"

2. You don't need to be attached to another human to be you. Your true personality, habits, and character traits are not based on another person's presence in your life. What you do and say and think must stand independent of anyone else. If there is anything that you only do or say or think when you are in a relationship, are you really that person? For example, if you only like football because the guy you're dating likes it, is that really who you are? If you only go to church because you're dating a church girl, is that really who you are? When we try to define our existence by the reaction we get from others, we betray our true self.

Day 9 Action: In your Bible read 2 Corinthians 12:9. In your journal answer, **in what areas of your life do you feel weak? In what ways do you see how God takes up the slack where you fall short?**

Day 10: In His presences is fullness of joy.

Everyone is either in a relationship, about to enter a relationship, or just got out of a relationship. If you experienced significant happiness in your previous relationship, you may find it hard to believe that you can be happy again apart from that connection. Looking back, it seems ridiculous that I actually believed I would never be happy again after the breakup. I think the problem was I so wanted to go to the next level in the relationship--to marriage---and I really thought if I just remained loyal, and tolerated all the stuff, it would happen. And once I got that ring, my dreams of limitless joy would come true. So I thought.

It is amazing what people associate with joy. Material and monetary wealth have been mistaken for success and joy for centuries. People believe that fame or lofty education will bring them joy. Although it isn't said out loud often, people even subconsciously believe that they will achieve joy when they completely control their lives. Most commonly, men and women alike believe that they will experience joy when they are in a relationship. And it's true. You will and you absolutely should feel great joy when you are in a healthy committed relationship with another healthy person. The flaw comes in when folks start to feel that they can only have joy when they are in a relationship in general, but not at all if they are single. When we start to replace the joy God gives with the happiness of man, this creates our conflict and sets up the great disappointment trap.

Happiness and joy are not the same thing. Happiness is based on circumstances. Joy is constant regardless of circumstances. Happiness ebbs and flows with the currents of life. Joy is rock solid, a force to be reckoned with. Happiness comes from the outside. Joy comes from the inside. The question is, how does one obtain this joy? Psalm 16:11 says,

"You will show me the path of life.; In Your presence is fullness of joy; at Your right hand are pleasures forevermore."

When I read these words during my recovery, I literally felt the healing begin to take place in my heart. I was lost and on a path of depression, but right here in the Word was the declaration I needed. God will show me the path of life, and my complete and full joy is found in His presence. No matter whether you are in a relationship or not, God's will is for you to have joy. This is a tricky concept to grasp because I know you're thinking, *what about when bad things happen?* Remember that joy is not based on happenings. It is based on the love of God. Jesus explained it this way,

> *"As the Father loved Me, I also have loved you; abide in My love. If you keep my commandments, you will abide in My love, just as I have kept my Father's commandments and abide in His love. These things I have spoken to you, that My joy may remain in you, and that your joy may be full." John 15:9-11*

So, the way to have joy is to abide in God's love and the way to abide in God's love is to keep His commandments. I hear you asking, *what are those commandments? Do you mean the Ten Commandments?* Well again, let's see what Jesus says about this.

> *"Jesus said to him, 'You shall love the Lord your God with all your heart, with all your soul, and with all your mind. This is the first and great commandment. And the second is like it: You shall love your neighbor as yourself. On these two commandments hang all the Law and the Prophets.'" Matthew 22:37-40*

All of the Ten Commandments, the Golden Rule, and everything in between can be attained in these two simple commandments. Love God and love others. Simple. Abiding in God's love is being in His presence where your joy is full and complete. That means everyday as you go about your tasks and your interactions with others, you are constantly dwelling in the love of God. It doesn't mean that you act weird or super spiritual. Rather, it means you have everlasting joy because you know and feel God's love for you and you know that nothing can ever take that away. Unlike my ex, God's love is not temperamental, and that gives me joy. After a breakup, our human nature wants to get even with the person who left us, broke us, and hurt us. Some people say the sweetest revenge is success. But I have learned through experience that success is shallow. The sweetest revenge is to not be bitter. The sweetest revenge *is* joy. Let it be the same for you.

Day 10 Action: One of the key ways I stay in God's presence is through worship. When I felt like crying in the shower, I decided to sing in the shower. It didn't always start off all that great. And I didn't feel good at the beginning. But after singing a few verses and the chorus of a praise and worship song my spirit began to feel lighter and lighter. Before I knew it, I was smiling and rejoicing in the Lord and feeling much better because I felt God's presence with me. King David is credited with being a man after God's own heart. I like to think that part of that is because David knew how to worship God and no matter what the situation was or even what David himself had done wrong, he knew that the secret to setting things right was through worship. Many of King David's psalms have been set to music or integrated into songs. Some of my favorites are listed below. Your task for today is to create your "In-His-Presence" soundtrack. What worships songs usher you into the Lord's presence? They can be old hymns, or contemporary worship songs. Where ever you listen to music, create a playlist of worship songs that bring your spirit into the presence of God where there is fullness of joy.

Psalm 9:1-2
I will praise You, O Lord, with my whole heart;
I will tell of all Your marvelous works.
I will be glad and rejoice in You;
I will sing praise to Your name, O Most High.

Psalm 103: 1-5
Bless the Lord, O my soul; And all that is within me,
Bless His holy name!
Bless the Lord, O my soul,
And forget not all His benefits:
Who forgives all your iniquities,
Who heals all your diseases,
Who redeems your life from destruction,
Who crowns you with lovingkindness and tender mercies,
Who satisfies your mouth with good things,
So that your youth is renewed like the eagle's.

Psalm 150
Praise the Lord!
Praise God in His Sanctuary; Praise Him in His Mighty firmament!
Praise Him for His mighty acts; Praise Him according to His excellent greatness!
Praise Him with the sound of the trumpet; Praise Him with the lute and harp!
Praise Him with the timbrel and dance; Praise Him with stringed instruments and flutes!
Praise Him with loud cymbals; Praise Him with crashing cymbals!
Let everything that has breath praise the Lord.
Praise the Lord!

Day 11: In Him you move, and breathe, and have your being.

I never could listen to the entire song. You know the one, "Unbreak My Heart." Even when my heart was broken, I could not bear the lyrics sung in the heartbreaking, deep tones of Toni Braxton. There were many days where I felt I could not breathe or move or think. My head was consumed with the loss and the disappointment. My body literally felt like a sack of rocks. These are all very strong signs of depression. No I wasn't suicidal, but my depression could have progressed into that state. There were still times where I struggled with just being able to function on a day-to-day basis, yet I was determined to get undumped.

The Apostle Paul explained to the ancient Greeks at Athens that God is in us, and we are in Him. Acts 17:28 says. *"...for in Him we live and move and have our being..."* It may seem strange, but really this is the only way we can survive when trouble comes into our lives, and whenever I felt like I could not take another moment, I reminded myself of this scripture. When I felt like I didn't have a reason to live or I didn't feel I could bear another minute, I remembered that I live IN HIM. My entire life is built on and based on the rock, Jesus Christ. Every move I make is in God, through God, and powered by God. My very existence is only possible because of God and what His Son Jesus did for me on the cross. This powered-by-God state does not go away just because you've had a breakup. Even though you may have felt like it, your ex is not the sun and the moon. He/She was not the source of your strength, and your next one won't be either.

When Christians take Communion, the minister usually reads the scriptures where Jesus instituted the practice. It was the same night that He was betrayed and arrested. But before that in a precious, tender, moment Jesus teaches His disciples how to practice communion by saying,

"Take eat, this is My body which is broken for you..." 1 Corinthians 11:24

Right now, your heart may be broken in a million pieces. You may be thinking of all the ways you need to just find someone new so that you can put this whole situation behind you. But I can assure you that no man or woman can unbreak your heart. Only Jesus can do that because He was broken for you.

Day 11 Action: In your journal draw a large heart and then divide it into sections like a puzzle. On each puzzle piece, write a word to describe a part of your heart you feel is broken due to your breakup. Then pray over your heart offering each broken piece to God for healing.

Say,

God, I come to You for healing and restoration of my broken heart. Your Word says in *Psalm 34:18* *"The Lord is near to those who have a broken heart…"* I trust that you are near me and in me even now Lord. I offer to you God each piece of my broken heart. Take it, heal it, and make it brand new. I surrender to Your capable hands and ask that You perform the open-heart surgery that I need to be whole. Show me the path of life. Help me to forgive my ex, and myself and please forgive me Lord, for my sins. Help me to accept your Agape love. I may not feel ready to open up fully to You right now, but I am willing. Help me to place You God as the head of my life and never let another person take Your place again. Thank You for hearing my prayer, and for already sending the answer. In Jesus' name, Amen.

Only Jesus can unbreak your heart, because He was broken for you.

Day 12: You are blessed and highly favored.

When you've experienced a breakup, it's hard to not feel as though you are damaged goods. Walking in the store one day, I saw something that helped me describe what I felt like after the breakup. On the "clearance" rack, items are discounted because they were returned and/or damaged in some way. A shirt may be missing a button. A zipper may not work. Or a pair of shoes were returned for being too small. I have to admit; this is what I felt like. Maybe you feel this way too. If you were the person dumped like I was, you probably feel as though there must be something wrong with you that made that person no longer want to be with you. If you were the person who chose to end the relationship, and dump your ex, you may feel frustrated that it didn't work out and still feel like the reason it didn't is because of some flaw in you. Whichever the case, here's what you need to know: You are not damaged goods. You are not a cracked coffee mug waiting on the clearance shelf for someone to pay $1 for you! *2 Corinthians 5:17 says, "Therefore if anyone is in Christ, he is a new creation; old things have passed away; behold, all things have become new."* No matter how bruised your breakup may have left you, you are all together new in Jesus Christ! But you must believe it. Take yourself off the clearance rack and see yourself as the precious child of God that you are. You are not a broken toy that no one wants. God wants you, and He gave His only Son to get you. There is no greater love!

Day 12 Action: In your Bible, read Ephesians 1:3-6. Look at verse 6 and underline or highlight the words "accepted in the Beloved." In your journal write out this declaration: "I am accepted in the Beloved by grace!" Repeat as often as needed until you believe that you are accepted by God. You are loved by God. You are blessed by God. No matter who left you or who you had to walk away from, you can never walk out of God's love for you.

You are not a cracked coffee mug waiting on the clearance shelf for someone to pay $1 for you!

Day 13: You were made for <u>more</u> than to be someone's girlfriend/boyfriend.

Following my divorce my main goal was to quickly remarry. For several flawed reasons, my entire focus was on securing a husband, despite being a single-parent, working full-time, and going to grad-school. Consequently, even though I thought I was in a very healthy state at the beginning of the ill-fated relationship, I was still strongly motivated by wanting to be married. There's an old song that says "you're nobody until somebody loves you." I believed that about myself to the core.

When you enter a relationship with tainted motives, it is bound to blowup in your face. I am not saying that you should not have engagement as a dating goal. But when that motive overrides every red flag and billboard sign warning you that this is not it, then there's a problem. This was my problem. I was so focused on getting the ring that I bulldozed right over his emotional state, and his wants and needs. I could not see that I had any other value but to be Mrs. Somebody, and it broke God's heart.

Yes, you read that last line correctly. I believe God was heartbroken over my choice to obsessively pursue marriage, ignoring the truth that I was created to be more than somebody's girlfriend/soon-to-be-hopefully-wife. Our society has over-sensationalized dating and relationships to the point that people have become obsessed with it. eHarmony, Match.com, BlackPeopleMeet.com and a host of other so-called dating sites perpetuate this frenzy of finding Mr./Mrs. Right. Our culture has created such a negative connotation with the word "single" that we treat it almost like a disease. We cannot stand to be by ourselves for even a moment. The thought of being alone drives us to unhealthy actions that carry devastating consequences. But being alone is not the problem of singleness. The frantic, psychotic, desperate rush to not be single is the problem.

It is like riding a merry-go-round. The circular motion of the merry-go-round causes riders to become dizzy and when you're a little kid that sensation feels weird and good at the same time. But the truth is that dizziness causes blurred vision, unstable steps, and even vomiting. This is exactly what going from relationship to relationship is like. The constant dating/relationship-merry-go-round will render you unable to see God's purpose for you, unable to walk in that purpose, and may even cause you to reject or throw-up your own purpose!

I used to feel that if I gave up looking for a mate, that dream would never be realized. I figured that as with most pursuits, I needed to work on this desire diligently, night and day, if I intended to see any results. What I didn't realize was that this mindset was preventing me from getting the very thing I wanted, and more importantly, it was not in-line with God's will for my life. Worrying about finding your soul mate is rooted in fear. God expressly instructs us to not be afraid and to not be anxious for anything, but to focus on your purpose. Jesus said it this way:

> *"Which of you by worrying, can add one cubit to his stature?"*
> *Matthew 6:27*

The Apostle Paul said it this way:

> *"Be anxious for nothing, but in everything by prayer and supplication, with thanksgiving, let your requests be made known to God, and the peace of God, which surpasses all understanding, will guard your hearts and minds through Christ Jesus. Philippians 4:6*

I believe that worrying about finding a mate is what drives people to make poor choices and poor decisions in dating and relationships. I know that was certainly the case for me. I was making decisions from a broken place rather than a healthy place. My selections in men were driven by selfish fear, instead generous love. To make matters worse, I only offered a shallow version of love which I thought would get me what I wanted in return. I tried to be the perfect girlfriend. I tried to stay calm about everything so that he wouldn't see me as a nagging, overly-emotional woman. I tried not to require priority standing in his life so that he wouldn't resent me. I offered sex so that he would know that I could satisfy him. I tried sweeping under-the-rug my intuition that was telling me there were some things wrong. I tried to avoid arguments, even at the expense of making things right in the relationship. None of it real agape love for that person. Just a means to an end really. But with all of that, the man dumped me anyway. Probably because he saw through my thinly-veiled ulterior motives. When you make decisions from a broken place every outcome of that choice will also be broken.

I chose to make searching for a mate my priority and that created more problems for me. But when you are focused on your purpose, and your purpose is the priority of your life, you are less prone to allow distractions or circumstances to derail you from your purpose. When God is the center of your life, every decision you make is made to be in-line with His purpose for you. You are empowered to weed out unhealthy relationship opportunities, not because of arrogance—I deserve this or that---but because you are protecting your destiny. Nowhere in the Word of God does it say that the number one pursuit in life is to be in a romantic, Eros relationship. This is not why man was created. You were made for more than to be someone's love interest.

Getting UnDumped!

You were deliberately created for a purpose; an imprint that you are supposed to leave on this world. It may be teaching in a classroom. It may be leading in a boardroom. Whatever it is, it does not begin or end with being someone's girlfriend/boyfriend.

You need to find out why God made you. What mission did He place inside you to carry out? He created you with a specific reason in mind that goes beyond just self-preservation, and when you diligently pursue that, you place matchmaking for you in God's hands, where it should be. God knew I wanted to be married. He heard me all 3,000 times I prayed about it. But God also knew that I wasn't ready for my true soul-mate because He will not give you a mate that you worship more than you worship Him. Do you know your purpose? Are you living your life in a way to best fulfill that purpose? Let's start today working on and figuring that out.

Day 13 Action:

1. Read---Psalm 37:4
2. Pray---Father God, I believe that you made me with a plan in mind that is greater than just being a girlfriend/boyfriend. Starting today, I want to live on purpose, instead of on the relationship merry-go-round. Show me what your plan is for my life and help me to follow

it. I believe that You know my heart's desires so as I focus on my purpose, I trust that you will bless me. In Jesus' name. Amen.

3. Listen---Listen for God to speak to you specifically about your purpose. Yes, He will talk to you. But you must quiet yourself and be patient. The main way that God speaks to us is through His Word. As you read God's Word daily you will receive revelations about what you have read. Find a daily Bible reading plan or a Bible study class. You will be surprised at the things that God reveals when you simply read, pray, and listen.

Day 14: Your relationship status does not determine your worth.

Filling out a simple questionnaire or application can be a painful experience when you're fresh out of a relationship. I stared at the bulleted check list contemplating which box I should mark:

- ☐ Single
- ☐ Married
- ☐ Divorced
- ☐ Other

I had attached self-worth values to each relationship status option. I thought that the only time it was acceptable to be single was during your 20's. At 35, I felt like some over-ripe fruit only good for the compost pile. I was no longer married. I was divorced, and in my mind at the time that was like being a cracked coffee-mug on the clearance shelf. I wasn't just single or divorced. I was in some awful, intangible, valueless, "other" category.

I've heard it said that you act upon what you truly believe. You can say anything you want, but the actions you take are based on what you believe in your heart. What I believed about myself was that without a man, I was absolutely of no value to anyone. I felt a lot of shame about the fact that I was a divorced, single-mother of three kids and it seemed as if everyone knew how much of a mess-up I was. Irrationally, I thought that with just one look at me, a person could tell that no one loved me. There were many days when wherever I went, all I seemed to see were all the happy dating or married women all around me. I would see a woman with a wedding ring set on and instantly think of how happy she was. How wonderful it must be to have someone in her life who cared about her, and protected her. How comforting to not have to go to the movies or out to eat alone, but to have a permanent companion. I would see women out with their boyfriends, clearly not married yet, but obviously on their way, so I thought in my head. Never mind the fact that these people were complete and total strangers to me. I knew absolutely nothing about them or their relationships whatsoever. All of my thoughts about them were based on me comparing myself to them. Comparing yourself to others is like playing Russian Roulette with a fully loaded gun. The result is a bullet straight to the head, every.single.time.

  During this second week of my breakup recovery, I had to readjust the foundation of my self-worth. Your self-worth cannot be based on something that fluctuates and changes periodically. When you do that, your worth is attached to the end of a roller-coaster where you are only valuable when you are in a relationship, but when you are not, you are useless. The reality is your romantic relationship status does not determine your worth. You are not better than anyone else when you are in a relationship, and you are not worse than everyone else when you are not in a relationship. This whole "at least I got a man," statement is really a cover-up for the larger problem of validation.

Validation does not come from Facebook "likes," or "good morning," texts, or that Louis Vuitton bag. You are valid because you are redeemed, Beloved. You were bought with a high price. Jesus laid down His life for you and there is no greater validation, no greater love than this! This is the only type of validation you can carry with you into any and every other relationship. Knowing that you belong to God and He loves you endlessly, will change the way you make decisions, the way you feel, the way you think and behave. I know you are thinking that God cannot hold you or make you feel like a human man or woman can. I thought that too. And I often pondered this quietly in my heart. I didn't want to be disrespectful, but I just could not see how God's love could replace the human love I needed. One day, He directly spoke to me concerning this.

What is it that you need so badly from a man that you are willing to give up so much of yourself, suffer abuse, accept lies and second-rate so-called love? You say you need verbal affection—you need the words. What greater words are there than Mine? You say you are afraid of being alone. Didn't I tell you <u>I will never leave you</u>?

You say I, God, cannot love you like a human man can. You don't know what I can do! You are not ready for Me to love you through a human man. Yes, you are broken in many places which has caused the many leaks in your heart. You must let me mend your heart before you will be able to even try to contain the amount of love I have for you.

~God

Day 14 Action: Your self-worth balance sheet. Businesses and corporations periodically pull a balance sheet to show the entity's value or net worth at a specific moment in time. You are a unique entity within yourself. Like a business, you do have assets (your personality, your heart, your love, your purpose), and liabilities (what you owe, but cannot pay), and when these two categories balance, the result is your net worth. However, unlike a business, your value does not decrease in the event of a breakup.

Your Self-Worth Balance Sheet

Assets: What Makes You Priceless	Liabilities: Unpayable by You
Your present life *"I have come that they may have life, and that they may have it more abundantly." John 10:10*	**Born into sin, you owed an unpayable debt,**
Your eternal life *"And this is eternal life, that they may know You, the only true God, and Jesus Christ whom You have sent." John 17:3*	**but God so loved you that He gave His Son,**
Your gifts and talents (Yes, you have some!) *But each one has his own gift from God, one in this manner and another in that. 1 Corinthians 7:7*	**Jesus, who died for you**
Your purpose *"For I know the thoughts I think toward you, says the Lord, thoughts of peace and not of evil, to give you a future and a hope." Jeremiah 29:11*	**and paid your debt.**

For a business, the way to compute the net worth is to subtract the liabilities from the assets and the remainder would be considered the net worth, simply speaking. Thankfully, that formula does not apply to your net worth because if it did, you and I would forever be in debt. But by accepting Christ, we enter the supernatural debt cancelation program. You are valid because you have purpose. You are valid because you are redeemed. You are a joint heir with Christ and you are worth more than millions! You are worth dying for! This is the definition of your value, and it has nothing, whatsoever, to do with your relationship status.

Jesus' blood sacrifice -- Your sin-debt = <u>Your Worth</u>

Wisdom

Week 3 What wisdom have you acquired from this experience?

Quite frankly, I didn't enter this relationship with the intent of learning anything. I am a teacher by profession, and I am the epitome of the ideal student, but I did not go into the relationship with notebook and pencil preparing to learn anything. I just wanted to be loved and cherished and of course, married. My true motivation for analyzing what had I learned from the experience was solely to avoid this pain in the future. What I have learned though, is that all of life is a teacher. The people who are successful in life are those who learn from every situation, every person, every high, every low. And when you know better, you should teach others, which is a big part of why you are holding this book right now. This last week of getting undumped was where I focused on reframing the picture of my past relationship and my present status. I will carry you through the same questions I asked myself to glean as much wisdom as I could to not make the same mistakes again in future relationships, but more importantly, to complete the healing process and be truly able to move on. Let us begin, shall we?

Each of the seven remaining days on this journey begin with one question that I ask you to ponder upon and then answer in your journal. Think carefully, about the questions. Don't rush ahead and try to do two or more questions at a time. Don't avoid a question that makes you a little uncomfortable. Answer them all. Instead of thinking only about what was wrong with the situation, look for what was right too. Tell yourself the truth. You deserve nothing less than the truth. And the truth will set you free *(John 8: 32)*.

Day 15 What was your emotional state before, during and after the relationship?

Go back to the day before the day you met him or her. Or, if you have known them since forever, go back to the day before the day you knew you were going to be together. How would you rate your emotional state then? Were you happy, complete and whole? Or did you feel like there was something missing, and then he/she stepped into your life and made your dreams come true? Were you in a spring season in your life where everything was new and fresh? Or were you in a fall season where everything was ending and dying? Did you enter your last relationship less than three weeks from the previous relationship? Had you been sort of talking to him/her before officially breaking up with your ex, ex? Were you screening every man/woman that walked by for boyfriend/girlfriend material, or were you not even looking for anybody at the time? Your emotional and mental state of mind just before embarking upon a new relationship adventure has a lot to do with who you choose and why you choose them, which ultimately has a lot to do with how the relationships goes and how it ends.

Next, think about your overall mental and emotional state through the duration of the relationship. Would you say it was happy and peaceful 80% or more of the time? Did you feel comfortable in their presence at all times? Or were you sometimes on edge, walking on egg shells trying to avoid upsetting them? Did you all handle conflicts fairly and maturely? Or did you behave childishly with episodes of the silent treatment, hanging up on each other in arguments, or being disrespectful to each other in public. Did you have real conflict resolution conversations where you were mutually heard and understood and a compromise was reached? Or did you use sex as a make-up tool after a fight and then just never spoke of the issue, until it came up again?

Finally, reflect upon how you felt right after the relationship ended. Were you devastated like I was? Did you try to immediately rectify the situation and get back together? Were you somewhat relieved at the breakup? I encourage you to take the time to write out your answers in your journal. It is not enough to just think about it in your head. Sometimes, the deepest, most life-changing things are revealed to us when we write. No, it is not just a woman thing! This book is not just for women. It is worth the time investment, after you think about it, to write out what was your emotional state before, during, and after the relationship.

Day 16 What were the fatal mistakes that led to the breakup?

This is not about blame. This is not about what you did wrong or what they didn't do at all. This is not about unforgiveness. This is simply about recognizing the fault lines. Fault lines are cracks in the Earth's crust that separate the Earth's tectonic plates. When the plates shift, sometimes earthquakes occur. Looking back now, were there active fault lines in your relationship? Was it just a matter of time before there was a clash that caused the split? Was everything going along great until one or more distinct events took place that blocked the love and halted the progress? There may be quite a few fatal mistakes, or there may just be one. Sometimes one is enough! Try to look past the typical differences that come up when dating that are minor. Look for the things that bothered you long after the fight about it was over. Or that issue that you never talked about for whatever reason. What were the things you or your ex said in the heat of an argument that opened a whole new can of worms because one or both of you didn't even know there was a problem, but the anger brought it to the surface? In your journal, today, write about the three (or more, or less) fatal mistakes that led to the breakup.

Day 17 What will you never do again?

"I will never wear that black dress again!" "I will never let my brother set me up with a woman again!" I can hear you saying these things! What *will* you never do again? Is it a certain outfit, or club, or restaurant? Is it the way you met the person, who introduced you, that you will never trust again? Why did you do the things you did that you now say you will not ever repeat? Did you feel that dress made you look sexy and therefore would attract attention? Did you hold your tongue and stuff your anger because you didn't know how to express it in a calm way and you didn't want to cause an argument? Did you accept a lie, or did you tell a lie? Did you stay in the relationship 5 months too long because you just didn't want to be alone? Did you jump in too fast because you just didn't want to be alone?

Essentially, what I am asking you is what are the things that you know better now or maybe you knew all along that you should not have done? I am asking you to analyze your motives behind why you did these things and compare that with why you are saying you will never do them again. Is it that you now know that sex outside of marriage is a sin? Is it that you knew that all along but did it anyway and now you see the problem it caused? Whatever it is, do not be ashamed at all! This is not about shame. This is about growth. This is not about regret. This is about the peace that comes from being wiser. What will you never do again and why? Share it in your journal.

Day 18 Who's on the Throne of Your Heart?

Deep in the tender chambers of your heart is a sacred throne room. It is plush with your velvet affections. Joy as sweet as the richest chocolate. Hate as dark as poison. Memories that haunt you live here, along with those that comfort you as well. The sky is speckled with kites of hope, while the ground is a forest of your heritage, upbringing, and culture. The throne room is heavily guarded by your daily, routine tasks, and distractions and the path to enter the room is the labyrinth of your life. In the center of this secret dormitory is a precious throne. There is room for only one person to sit on the throne at a time. When the throne is occupied, all other suitors must wait until YOU choose to remove and/or replace the Lord of Your Heart, and whoever sits on the throne of your heart, rules your life.

When your job, your kids, your money, your desire for money, or your girlfriend/boyfriend sit on the throne of your heart, that is what directs and dictates all that you do and say and feel. If it's your job, then you tend to be a workaholic, out of balance emotionally and sometimes physically. If it's the drive for money, there is usually little room for compassion for others. If it's your significant other, you seriously compromise your emotional health and well-being. The only one that has the grace to sit on the throne of your heart, without negative effects to you is Jesus Christ. When Jesus is the Lord of your life everything else will fall into its rightful place. Your priorities will be in the proper order. You will be able to maintain emotional balance. I don't mean to say that this will all instantly happen, but as you choose to place Jesus on the throne of your heart every day, your life will be in order and you will experience peace and joy through even the darkest storms. Placing a human, love interest on the throne of your heart will inevitably end with you getting dumped or at best, living beneath God's desire for you. In fact, the best gift you can give yourself in your next relationship, is to keep Jesus on the throne of your heart, and you will have plenty of love to give away too! In your journal, write a letter to the One who sits on the throne of your heart.

Day 20 What is God telling you now?

At this point in this journey you should be getting a little more familiar with God's voice if you were not before, or perhaps this has been a refresher for you if somewhere along the way you drifted from His side. Either way, there is no better time than right now, to incline your ears and your heart to hear from your Heavenly Father. My prayer is that God has been speaking to you all throughout this book and I pray mostly, that you have been paying attention. I could tell you all the things God has shared with me but that may not perfectly align with or apply to your life. God would so much rather have a personal one-on-one conversation with you Himself. So, for today I would like you to read the scriptures listed below, pray the prayer, and then listen for what God says to you.

1. Read---Proverbs 3:5-6; Psalm 37:7, 1 Kings 19:11-12;
2. Pray—Dear God, thank you for the privilege of being able to talk with you and knowing that you hear me. I may not have always heard your voice or even believed that you do speak to people but I am putting forth my faith to hear you now. I am asking you now God to direct me in what I should do concerning my heart and relationships. Guide me Lord in romantic matters so that I do not cause pain nor experience

unnecessary pain. Help me to see the real motives in people who are attracted to me. Help me to seek companionship for the right reasons from a healthy heart and not a broken one. Speak to me Lord, and help me to recognize your still, small, voice so that when the next person comes along, I will hear clearly from you. In Jesus' name, Amen.

3. Listen---take a moment to pause, and listen quietly. Don't get caught up expecting to hear an audible voice speak to you, although God could absolutely do that if He wanted. But also, just pay attention to what thoughts come to mind now that you've prayed. Are there any messages from anywhere in this book that come back to your memory? That could be God speaking to you. Whatever you hear in your heart, write it in your journal.

Day 21 What will you do differently?

There is a saying that says "The definition of insanity is to do the same thing over and over again, expecting different results." If you bring the same you to the next relationship, you are most likely going to end up in the same situation because YOU are the common denominator. So what are you going to do differently? Yes, you will most likely be in another relationship. Do not even entertain thoughts that you will be lonely and single for the rest of your life. We already took care of that earlier in this book. Don't go back into that bondage again. So when the next potential "One" appears in your life, what are you going to do that is different from what you've done before? I am not talking about revamping your whole personality to suit someone and make them like you. That almost never works and they won't like you simply because you were not genuinely you. Instead, I mean for you to be the wise advisor to your future, beautiful self, having experienced a breakup and come out on the other side. What do you know now that you didn't know before? About yourself? About God? About love? How will you use this knowledge to make better choices in every area of your life? There is nothing you can do about the past, but there is a whole lot you can do about the future. You don't have to be stuck in the dumps because the love that you thought was going to be a "couple of forevers" did not work out that way. The best way to get over someone is not with someone else. The best way to get over someone is to declare to yourself what mistakes you will not repeat and what positive steps you will take so that you can be relationship healthy and whole. Finally, on this 21st day of this 3-week journey, write in your journal what you are going to do differently.

Epilogue: *What I Learned*

It's been quite a journey to **#GettingUnDumped**, and even though I may not know you personally, I feel like we have been through something major together. I've shared with you one of the worst time periods of my life where I really struggled, but God enabled me to get back up from being knocked down and move forward. I pray with all my heart that you were encouraged, inspired, and experienced healing as a result of reading this book. Thank you so much for taking the time to do so.

My desire is for you to learn from my mistakes and pitfalls, as well as my faith and my triumphs. I never wanted this book to be just a memoir of my bad breakup because other than sharing the pain, that would be of little value to you. I wanted you to learn and grow from your own bad experience with more than just a "I did it, so can you," type of book. I wanted to give you practical tools and most of all point you to the ultimate healer, Jesus Christ. There are some things that I will share in this epilogue that I learned, that were specific to my situation and perhaps you will be blessed here as well. Maybe you will see yourself in me and if that can help you in anyway, then the pain was not in vain for me. God bless you, Beloved!

What was your emotional state before, during and after the relationship?

Before I met the gentleman who dumped me, I was not looking for a man. After my divorce, I had crashed and burned through a handful of frogs, toads, and snakes (smile) so I was in that "I don't need a man," state. He was in a relationship--engaged no less--so I thought I was playing it safe by giving him relationship advice to help him with his "cold feet." I truly was not interested in him and I thought I was getting practice for becoming a relationships coach with him. So when he called me out of the blue and told me that he called off the wedding and moved out of the apartment with his fiancé, I was more than shocked. But I figured that it was because their relationship just wasn't working because we had talked about some major red flags with that situation. I had no idea that he had his eyes set on me. To this day, I am not really sure what he was thinking at the time. Later, his ex-fiancé would call me to let me have a piece of her mind! Lesson for the day: Don't ignore the red flags presented at the beginning of the relationship. If he is fresh out of a relationship, especially an engagement, he is emotionally unavailable for a real relationship with you.

What were the fatal mistakes that led to the breakup?

In my break-up, one of the things I was angry about was his response to my question about marriage. Well, it wasn't really a question...let me explain. Like many of you, I had heard the advice that you should state your relationship intentions early and a real man would also be clear about his intentions right from the start. I had read that I should have standards and make those standards clear upfront so that there would be no confusion later. So, in that cloudy mindset, I set out to do that in this relationship. In a casual conversation, I let him know that my intentions were to eventually get married. I did not want to be someone's permanent girlfriend. I was too old for that! And I said to him with an air of arrogance quite frankly, "If you don't see yourself getting married anytime soon, let me know now and we can go our separate ways as friends, no hurt feelings." There. I had done it. I had set out my intentions and made my standards clear. I would not be taken advantage of this time! And what was his response? Surprisingly, he did not immediately drop to one knee and propose right there. He simply said "I can respect that." Lesson of the day: Don't misinterpret what he says and then create a whole complete fantasy world based on your misconception. I heard what I wanted to hear and perpetrated the story in my head despite having no outside evidence to support it. When a man is ready to marry, he will make definite plans and moves in that direction. You won't have to guess. I know that for certain now. That is exactly what my husband did!

What will you do differently?

I honestly could write a whole other book about this alone! There were so many mistakes I made, not just in this particular relationship, but all the ones before it including my first marriage. "What are you going to do differently," is the question I challenge myself with regularly and whenever I am in an unpleasant situation. I believe that if we all paused at the end of each day and asked ourselves this question in preparation for the next day, the world would be a better place indeed! Probably one of the most important things I vowed to do differently was to stop believing that I was damaged goods from being divorced, and that I needed a relationship to prove my worth. I vowed to think differently. As I have said in this book, people can say a lot of things but they act on what they believe. I had to stop believing that I was worthless, because I saw how that was the root cause for so many of my poor choices in men. I believed that I had to earn their love. I believed that I did not deserve for anyone to love me genuinely and completely. I believed that I had to be superwoman to keep a man from cheating on me. I believed that God could not care less about my love life and I would be lucky if I found anyone who would even consider marrying me. Every one of my mistakes can probably be traced back to one of these flawed beliefs. The shift in my thinking brought about the change I needed in my life. The Bible says "we are transformed by the renewing of our minds," (Romans 12:2). This is what worked for me, and this is what I tried to impart to you in this book.

Again, thank you so much for taking the time to read this. God bless you. I love you all,

Joy

Appendix A: The Secret to Getting UnDumped

The greatest decision you can make in your whole life is making Jesus Christ the Lord of your life. If you followed the prayer to do this from Week 1, Day 6, you are:

- Forgiven,
- A child of God, and
- You have eternal life!

But that doesn't mean that you're done. Your lovely journey is just beginning. Just like a romantic relationship, your relationship with Jesus Christ takes work. You have to communicate and build trust. The way to do that is:

- Pray to God daily (read John 15:7)
- Read God's word daily (read Acts 17:11)
- Obey God every moment (read John 14:21)
- Allow God to transform your life (read 1 Peter 5:7)
- Receive the gift of the Holy Spirit (read Galatians 5:16, 17)

Life as a Christian is not meant to be done alone or in isolation. You need a tribe, a family of believers that will encourage you, uplift you, and who knows? You may even meet your soulmate! (smile!) So, if you are not a member of a church, do not delay to reach out to a local church where the death, burial, and resurrection of Jesus Christ is preached. Many churches have a website where you can read about their beliefs and find out their service times, and contact information. Find out when the next service is and go! Keep going and trying different churches until you hear God tell you where you should plant roots and join.

I'd love to know that you received Jesus as a result of reading this book. Please go to www.joyrrobinson.com to share your testimony with me and receive a gift!